Marketing Yourself

Strategies to promote your editorial business

Fourth edition

Erin Brenner and Sara Hulse

Published in the UK in 2023 by
Chartered Institute of Editing and Proofreading
Studio 206, Milton Keynes Business Centre
Foxhunter Drive, Linford Wood
Milton Keynes
Buckinghamshire
MK14 6GD

ciep.uk

Copyright © 2023 Chartered Institute of Editing and Proofreading and Sara Hulse

ISBN 978 1 915141 18 7 (print)
ISBN 978 1 915141 19 4 (PDF ebook)
ISBN 978 1 915141 20 0 (ePub)

Fourth edition

First published by the SfEP as Developing a Marketing Strategy 2008
Second edition 2013, ISBN 978 0 9563164 7 9, reprinted 2016
Third edition 2018, ISBN 978 0 9931293 2 2 (print) and 978 0 9931293 6 0 (ebook)

All rights reserved. No part of this publication may be reproduced or used in any manner without written permission from the publisher, except for quoting brief passages in a review.

The moral rights of the authors have been asserted.

The information in this work is accurate and current at the time of publication to the best of the authors' and publisher's knowledge, but it has been written as a summary or short introduction only. Readers are advised to take further steps to ensure the correctness, sufficiency or completeness of this information for their own purposes.

Typeset in-house
Original design by Ave Design (**avedesignstudio.com**)
Image credits: Pixabay, Shutterstock and Unsplash

Contents

1	Why do you need a marketing plan?	1
2	Reviewing your business and crafting a brand	3
	Identifying and targeting clients	3
	Determining how you uniquely meet your clients' needs	5
	Crafting a distinctive brand	6
3	Choosing marketing methods that are right for you	10
	Basic marketing materials	11
	A business website	14
	Directories	16
	Advertising	17
	Cold calling: Letters, emails and phone calls	18
	Networking	21
	Social media	24
	Online events	25
	Building relationships with your clients	26
4	Putting your plan together	29
5	Implementing your plan and measuring its effectiveness	33

Appendix 1 | A basic checklist   36

Appendix 2 | Resources   38
    CIEP resources   38
    Further learning and advice   38
    Professional directories   38
    Business support and networking organisations   39

1 | Why do you need a marketing plan?

As an editorial freelancer you may think that marketing isn't relevant to you, but it's vital to think of yourself as a business owner who is offering a service or range of services.

Business owners use marketing plans to create brand recognition among their desired clients and to generate leads.

In other words, they need their potential clients to know who they are and what they do, and they need clients to contact them when they are ready to buy.

As a freelance editor, you, too, need your potential clients to know who you are and what you do. How else can they know to hire you? Whether you're just starting in freelance editing or you've been doing it for a while, this guide is designed to give you ideas for (re)creating your marketing plan.

Your marketing plan contains your approach to marketing and the steps you'll use to put your plan into action. Whether you use a template or write your plan from scratch, your plan should be uniquely suited to your business. It should detail whom you intend to target and how you'll let them know about your services – hopefully without spending a fortune.

Maybe you're perfectly happy with the amount of work you have and with your current clients. But don't forget that every year, through no fault of your own, you'll likely lose a number of your clients through relocation, competition, change of business, closure or contacts moving on. Even to stay still, you need to have some way of replacing these clients. You need to protect yourself from future changes in the market, such as a publisher taking all of its proofreading work in-house or sending it overseas.

Many of us are guilty of relying on a small number of clients and on word of mouth to gain new clients. If we do any marketing at all, it tends to be reactive and sporadic. As you go through the process of creating a marketing plan for your business, keep in mind that marketing is not a one-off activity but rather an ongoing process. Your marketing efforts should focus on getting plenty of new clients coming in, lots of inactive clients coming back and all your current clients using you more.

2 | Reviewing your business and crafting a brand

The first step is to review your current situation – define your business as it stands now and assess your personal strengths, skills and resources. What services do you offer? Be very clear about this and about what you can and can't do. What are your areas of expertise? Could you learn new skills in order to offer a wider range of services?

Clients may think editing is editing; it doesn't matter who you hire. Editors know better. Think about what makes you a good fit for your desired clients. What makes you unique? For example, are you able to turn work around quickly or to work in-house? Do you offer a related service, such as project management? How do you stand apart from other editors?

Identifying and targeting clients

What kind of clients do you want to work for? By defining who your clients are, you'll be in a better position to create a plan for finding them. We'd all like clients who pay on time, offer good rates and value what we do. We can consider that as given. Who are your clients specifically?

Start with the basics:

- Are your desired clients individuals or organisations?
- What kind of materials do they need edited?
- What level of editing is needed?

Then add detail to who your clients are:

- How well do they understand the editing process? What do they need to be educated about?

- If they're organisations, are they big or small? What industry do they work in? Do they have a niche or a speciality?
- What's the job title of the person who would hire you? What's their role in their organisation? What are some of the obstacles they face in publishing the materials you'd edit?
- What topics do your clients write about?
- If they're individuals, are they planning to publish traditionally or self-publish? If they're not planning to publish at all, why do they write and why does quality matter?
- For fiction clients, what kind of fiction do they write? For poetry clients, what kind of poetry do they write?

Use these questions to inspire you to come up with more questions. Create as detailed an image of your clients as you can.

> **Tip**
>
> Write a description of your ideal client. If you have current clients who fit your ideal, look at them closely. The more you know whom you're trying to attract, the better you'll know how to go about persuading them to hire you.

Do you work with different types of clients? You may need to develop a different marketing approach for each. For example, if you edit reports for companies and theses for doctoral students, you may want to emphasise different knowledge and skills to each. Think about the particular challenges each client faces and how you can help overcome them – whether that might be turning work around quickly and at short notice, making use of specialist subject knowledge or guiding clients through the self-publishing process.

Clients like to work with freelancers who inspire confidence. As a freelancer, you may feel like a passive party, waiting humbly for the all-powerful client to give you some work. But for a client, the most appealing freelancers are those who are confident in their skills and are able to empathise with their needs.

Determining how you uniquely meet your clients' needs

Editorial freelancers are no different from other small businesses. Even if you work alone and operate as a sole trader, you still need to develop a professional business image. What makes you the best choice for your clients? What can you do that no one else can?

Marketers often call the answers to these questions your 'unique selling proposition' (USP). You'll use your USP to let your ideal client know that you're the right person for them. You'll communicate your understanding of their needs, as well as how you meet those needs.

Your USP might include expertise in your client's subject or the ability to complete the project faster than other editors might. Maybe you're willing to edit AI-created copy or work in the client's proprietary system. Think about how you typically work and how that might benefit your clients.

> **Tip**
> Receiving feedback on your work can help you better understand your clients' needs and the specific role you play in fulfilling them. But clients rarely give feedback without prompting! Ask current or past clients what they like about working with you or how you helped them. You might even create a feedback survey that you can share at the end of every job to continue collecting feedback. Any answers you receive can help you determine why people value working with you in particular.

Through this research you'll build up a picture of your ideal clients, what their particular needs are and how you can meet those needs. With that, you're ready to create a plan to find those clients.

Crafting a distinctive brand

Next, you'll want to develop a brand – a way for people to remember who you are and something distinctive about you. It will focus on your USP, your values, your service and your clients.

Elevator pitch

Start with a clear, concise and memorable message that communicates what you do. You can incorporate everything you've been researching and collecting about your business up to this point, including your USP, but remember that you'll need to condense it to a few sentences. This is often called an 'elevator pitch' because you should be able to share the message in a short lift ride. Here are examples from a few CIEP members (including one of the authors):

- I'm a copyeditor and proofreader working across both fiction and non-fiction. In fiction, I specialise in fantasy, science fiction, YA, romance, contemporary fiction, and horror. I'm happy to work on non-conventional texts. In non-fiction, I specialise in the arts, humanities, social sciences, self-help, and lifestyle. I have a lot of experience working with self-publishing authors as well as directly with publishers. I have also worked on essays, dissertations, theses, and business content (web pages, promotional material, and so on).
  – Catherine Dunn

- I offer professional, friendly and personalised editorial support and have worked on PhD theses, master's dissertations and academic journal papers, book chapters, blog essays and travel writing, business documents, magazine articles and content for web pages. I have helped a variety of clients to ensure that their written material is free from errors and consistent in content and presentation, including the formulation of style sheets and guides where necessary.
  – Rachel Duncan

- I work as a developmental editor, copyeditor, and proofreader for independent clients as well as publishers, having edited more than 100 books. These works have spanned genres from romance to crime and historical fiction to psychology non-fiction. My specialty, though, is speculative fiction, including fantasy, magical realism, fabulism and science fiction. Any story with a bit of the strange, the magical, the fantastic: that's my area.
  – Laura Burge

- Right Touch Editing provides small and midsized businesses with freelance editors to help increase writing quality and put projects back on track. We work on a variety of business copy, including internal reports, marketing content, and product documentation. Your freelance team will specialise in your topic. They're available now and scalable at any time.
  – Erin Brenner

You may need slightly different versions of this message for different types of clients. Let's say you copyedit for both publishing houses and self-publishing authors. Publishing houses know what copyeditors do, have processes for working with them and usually have set budgets. You might want to highlight your experience working with other publishing houses, any bestsellers you've worked on or something else that makes you valuable to these clients.

Self-publishing authors, however, may need a lot more education on what editing is, the different types of editing, the publishing process, fees for these services and more. In your messaging you might highlight the extra support you offer these clients or the service packages you provide that are designed to help them save money.

Make sure you also promote your ancillary skills. Someone may appreciate your marketing, administrative, teaching or IT skills as well as your proofreading and editing ones, especially outside book publishing. Be confident – bring what you know to the table and don't be shy about selling it.

> **Tip**
>
> Test out your elevator pitch on friends and family. Do they understand what you're trying to say? Are you able to share it within 30 seconds or so – without speed-talking? Keep working at it until you find a message that is clear and that you feel comfortable with.

Tagline

An even shorter message you can consider creating is the tagline, or slogan. This brief message will often pair with your logo and is short enough to put on business cards, in social media profiles and in other small places. It should be easy to remember and communicate the core idea of your business. Here are a few examples from fellow editors:

Swanford Editorial Services Limited (Petra Roberts): Efficient medical editing

What I Mean To Say (Maya Berger): Editorial services for authors and business data expertise for editors

Heather Musk Editorial: Proofreading and copyediting for science fiction, fantasy and speculative fiction authors

Logo

You may want to develop a logo for your business as well. You'll want to put a good deal of thought into it and maybe work with a designer to ensure it looks professional. This small image needs to be memorable and communicate the core idea of your business. Use your logo everywhere you can: business cards, other stationery, website, invoices – anywhere that you can put a logo or image.

Design features

Also think about typefaces and colours to represent your business. Both should be incorporated into your logo and be used to create your branding materials, especially your website. Again, consulting a logo or brand designer can be a good investment for your business.

Head shot

As a business owner, try to avoid being camera-shy. A professional photo of you can be used as part of your branding and helps clients see you as a real person. While hiring a photographer can help you get results you're pleased with, you can have a friend take one or use a quality selfie. The best head shots are head and shoulders only, with neutral backgrounds. Be sure you look professional or otherwise represent your brand. Remember that a lot of the places you'll put your head shot, like on social media profiles, will display only thumbnails. You want your image to be recognisable at a small size.

Not everyone is comfortable with sharing their photos, however. If it's really not for you, you can create an avatar that fits in with your brand or use your logo instead.

3 | Choosing marketing methods that are right for you

This step requires some brainstorming and research. But if you're clear about your capabilities and what you're trying to achieve, the decision about how to promote yourself and your business most effectively becomes easier.

For inspiration, look at your existing connections with other freelancers. What are they doing to market their businesses?

Obviously you don't want to copy exactly anything that someone else is doing, but you can certainly create a version that fits your business.

You can follow other editors on social media outlets, subscribe to their newsletters and surf around their websites. Learn how they share information on these networks, the types of information they share and when they share it. You can learn a lot from your fellow editorial professionals.

Remember: some marketing methods will work better for you than others, and even different approaches will work better at different stages of a business. Early on, advertising on directory websites might give you a good start, but later on you may find that most of your jobs come from existing clients and colleagues.

Basic marketing materials

What materials should you have ready to share with potential clients? You have several to choose from. Choose as many as you like.

CV

Whether you need a CV will depend on the type of clients you have, but it's always a good idea to have one you can share at a moment's notice.

As a freelancer, you want a functional, or skills-based, CV to promote your skills, training and accomplishments. List a sampling of current and past clients, taking care not to list those you are contractually not allowed to. These things will reassure potential clients that you can do the work on offer. Review your CV annually for any updates.

Be sure to create a format you can tweak quickly to fit different types of clients and consider creating a few of the more common formats to have on hand, such as Word, text-only (to copy into online forms) and PDF. Whatever formats you choose, make sure they look professional and don't contain errors. You can use a CV-building website to help create a visually appealing document. Consider asking or hiring a fellow editor to edit your CV for you.

Business cards

Depending on who your clients are and the type of in-person networking you do, you may want to have business cards. Your business card should state clearly who you are and give a good indication of what you do – because people will forget. If someone picks up your business card again a year after they've met you, your name and even the name of your business might not be enough to convey exactly what you do.

Naturally, you'll want to include your contact details, such as email address, mobile number and website address. Consider adding a QR code that goes to your website or other online location. When one of these contact points changes, get new cards. Writing in new information is often perceived as unprofessional.

> **Tip**
>
> Always carry your business cards with you and hand them out at every opportunity. It's amazing where they end up, and they can sometimes produce work from the unlikeliest of sources. They're a cheap way to get information about yourself and your business out to the wider world.

You don't need to spend a lot of money on business cards. There are many options for printing something professional-looking for less; research the latest options or ask other freelancers what they use. You also don't need to purchase hundreds of cards if you don't anticipate handing them all out or you think you'll need to update the cards soon. Small batches are available from many vendors.

Virtual business cards

You can create virtual business cards instead of or to supplement your printed business cards. A virtual business card is essentially a digital space, such as a webpage or entry in an app, where your contact information is listed, often with options to add your image, logo and other branding elements. You might share your virtual business card through a URL, QR code, app or physical object, such as a card people can scan with their phones. Not only does a virtual business card allow you to share a lot of contact information virtually but it's easier to update than printed cards.

Brochures

Would your clients benefit from reading a brochure or other visual presentation that explains who you are, what you do and how they would benefit from working with you? For clients who need to know more about you or the publishing process, a branded brochure can help persuade them that you're the right person for the job.

At minimum, your brochure should answer a prospective client's basic questions. Detail the services you offer, who your typical clients are and what it's like to work with you. Talk with your clients: what results have they seen from working with you? For example, if a book you edited wins an award, you can promote the fact that you worked on it. Or if a client reports that they received a grant through the grant application you worked on, you can share that. Just be careful not to promise results. Editors don't control the copy after it's left our hands, and other factors go into the results any writing project achieves.

Don't forget to include a brief bio of yourself and your contact information. Include your head shot, if you have one, and make sure any other images fit your brand.

You don't have to know a lot about design to create a brochure, though a little knowledge helps. Tools like Canva have templates that you can start from, and the customisation options are nearly limitless. Keep your brand design in mind when choosing typefaces, colours, images and design elements. The more a brochure looks like your brand, the stronger the identification will be for your ideal clients.

You can offer your brochure digitally as a free download from your website or in response to people with basic enquiries about your service. All of these can save you time by giving prospective clients just starting their research a way to get to know you without a long email or phone conversation.

Printing brochures can be expensive, so shop around if you're going to do it and think about how many copies you'll actually need. If you'll be able to give them out at an event where your clients will be, it could be worth the cost. People will have something tangible to take away with them. But if you rarely meet prospective clients or colleagues in person, print could be a waste of money, especially if your business card will work as well. A QR code on your business card that leads to your digital brochure can bridge the gap.

A business website

There's no doubt that prospective clients will search for your website. It's a rare business that doesn't have some sort of an online presence, especially because there are so many tools that make setting up a website easy. Your website lends you professional authority, makes you easy to find, shows that you use current technology and lets you tell a more in-depth and up-to-date story about your business than a CV or brochure can. You can include information about recent projects, your skills and qualifications, the nature of the work you're seeking, your business terms and conditions and so much more.

It's a rare business that doesn't have some sort of an online presence

Your clients may be starting with a broad web search for an editor, or they may be finding you in other ways, with the website being a later stop on their journey to hiring you. They might visit to research you, verifying that you're legitimate and have the right skills. They might want to get a better understanding of the services you offer and for whom. Or they might want to get a sense of who you are and whether you'd be a good fit for their project.

If you want to use your website as a way to draw in new clients, you'll need to put information on your site that they're looking for. Think about what needs your client has that relate to your editing service. This could be informative articles on self-publishing, a blog on changes in language use, lists of other publishing professionals your client might need – whatever you can imagine.

Even with all the tools available, creating and maintaining a professional-looking website takes time, and it will need regular reviewing and updating. The costs depend on your time and skills and how big or complex a site you choose to make. If you don't have a large budget for website design or copywriting, you don't have to go completely without. Some website hosts offer free templates you can use to create your site, and you can choose to create a smaller site to reduce the work.

You could also trade skills. If you know a website designer, for example, perhaps they could design your website at a discounted rate in exchange for you proofreading website content for their clients.

Ideally your website's domain name (the bit between the *www* and the *com*, *co.uk* or other ending) should be your business name, though that's not always possible. Think, too, about how your name reads without spaces to avoid embarrassing misreading. When your business name isn't possible or practical, try for something memorable and related to who you are or what you do.

> **Tip**
>
> Once you have a domain name, set up an email address that uses it. It's worth the extra cost for the unified, professional look. It tells clients that you didn't just set up a throwaway free email account; you're an established, trustworthy business.

Writing copy for the web is a particular skill. If you don't have experience in this area, then it's worth spending part of your budget on having it done professionally. If you opt to do it yourself, make sure you get some sort of objective, external review of your work. Look at the websites of other freelancers to get inspiration (but obviously don't copy their ideas). And ask editing colleagues if they'd be willing to trade editing services, helping both of you publish higher-quality sites.

Directories

The CIEP Directory is a popular first stop in many clients' search for a freelance editor, so upgrading your membership to Professional or Advanced Professional is worthwhile, if you haven't done so already. If you're an Intermediate Member, don't forget that you can be listed in IM Available, another valuable means of getting work.

Check out other professional organisations with directories that you are eligible to join. For example, your local chamber of commerce and your clients' industry organisations, as well as other editing organisations, such as Editors Canada, the Institute of Professional Editors and the Editorial Freelancers Association.

> **Tip**
> Think about the industries you commonly work in, the area you live in, and the services you offer to help you find appropriate organisations to join. Don't forget alumni associations for the schools, colleges or universities you attended.

Some people seem to get a steady stream of work from key directories and listings, but few seem to rely on them as a primary marketing tool. Competition is high, so make your entry stand out. Be clever about what you say about yourself, and use keywords to highlight your skills rather than lengthy text. Mention, too, the areas in which you have experience and expertise. Look at existing entries to see what's effective and eye-catching. Avoid saying that you can work on anything, even if you're a generalist; clients want to know you can work on their type of project. Give them examples of the work you do.

Advertising

Whether print or digital, advertising is generally an expensive method of marketing. To make the cost and effort worthwhile, carefully consider who will see your advert and how close they are to hiring an editor. You want to ensure that your ideal clients will see it and that they're ready to hire.

If you edit for self-publishing fiction authors, for example, an advert in the Alliance of Independent Authors' membership directory (separate from your member entry) or the member magazine might be valuable to you. An advert in a local guide or bulletin might be less so.

Digital adverts, such as those found on Google, Facebook and other popular locations, can offer the opportunity to closely define who will see the advert and put an affordable cap on costs. But will it be shown often enough for people to remember your business and contact you? Sometimes the only way to know is to test it, spending only as much as you're willing to throw away.

When it comes to creating the adverts themselves, you may find that the place where you'll advertise will create the advert for you. You hand them your logo and the text, and they do the rest. Others will want you to supply the art. A tool like Canva may help you avoid hiring a costly designer. Still others will have tools for advertisers to use to create adverts, as Meta does.

However you approach advert creation, make sure to check the final proof. Check that everything is spelled correctly, your logo and other art display correctly and the overall look represents your business well.

Cold calling: Letters, emails and phone calls

Cold calling is probably the least favourite marketing method among freelancers. If you can do it, it can bring rewards, but be prepared for a lot of point-blank refusals, people who don't really know what you're talking about and repeated efforts to reach the person you want.

Start by researching companies that you might be a good fit for. Ensure you have the desired specialised knowledge, skills and experience to perform the service the company needs. It would damage your brand if you won an opportunity to work for a new client only to demonstrate that you're not qualified to do so.

You'll want to reach the person in charge of hiring a freelance editor. If it's not clear on the website, try asking someone in HR or a receptionist. A misdirected contact will very likely be ignored.

Next, determine how you will reach out to prospective clients. The following are three common methods.

Letters

Posting a cover letter and CV or a well-designed brochure can catch someone's attention because so much outreach is done via email. Posting letters could get expensive if you contact everyone this way, and there's no way to know if your letter actually reaches the correct person (more on that below). But it could well be worth standing out from the crowd.

3 | Choosing marketing methods that are right for you

Make sure your materials clearly show how you are the right choice for the company. Use your skills-based CV (discussed earlier), and develop a cover letter that you can easily adapt to different client types and different contact methods. And of course, make sure you've proofed your materials carefully.

Email

By far the most common method currently used, email offers many benefits. It can be easier to track down email addresses, you will be alerted if your message is undeliverable and a follow-up message can be sent with the original message. The downside is the real possibility of getting lost in someone's inbox or being mistakenly relegated to the spam folder.

The email's subject line will help you stand out in someone's bulging inbox. Craft a subject line that gets the reader's attention by highlighting the solution to the problem you solve (eg booking an editor on short notice), the outcome of working with you (eg increased quality) or perhaps something intriguing (eg your USP or a personal connection you have to the client's work).

Be sure, too, that your subject line is within 60 characters, including spaces. This helps ensure the whole subject line is visible in different email software. Email best practices are always evolving, so be sure to research the latest thinking when crafting your emails.

Phone

Cold phone calls are less frequent than they once were, but done well they can be successful, especially if you develop a thick skin for a lot of rejection. When making a call, make sure you're in a quiet location, you have a script in front of you, you have a strong signal and you're calling during the company's normal business hours.

Having a script can help calm nerves and ensure you make the points you want. After briefly introducing yourself and giving the reason for your call, ask whether this is a good time for them. If it is, continue with your script, but don't read from it. You'll want to practise it enough that it becomes a guide for you and you can speak naturally and confidently.

If it's not a good time for a call, ask what a better time might be or offer to email them instead.

If you get voicemail, be brief and professional. Give your phone number and/or email address slowly and clearly – but don't expect them to call you back. Plan to call again at another time.

Be professional and brief

No matter how you reach out, keep your message brief and high level. Focus on the client's needs and how you can fulfil them, and mention anyone you have in common. *Don't* mention your need for work; it can be off-putting. Instead describe (briefly) your skills and experience and how that would help them. On a call, offer to email them a link to your website or your CV. In an email, share the link to your site and offer to follow up with a CV (avoiding any wariness of opening an unexpected file from a stranger).

You can build a little trust and goodwill by sharing your willingness to:

- take an editing test
- start with a later stage of editing, such as proofreading instead of copyediting
- fill in for a regular freelancer
- do a trial project
- do a rush job.

Being flexible in order to help a busy staff member is a great way to get started with a new client.

If you don't reach the right person or get a response on the first try, by all means follow up but take care not to overwhelm them with repeated follow-ups. Limit yourself to just one or two follow-ups.

> **Tip**
>
> Track your cold-calling efforts. Record the company, contact person and contact details, date you reached out, the method you used, the result and any follow-up plan. If you've told your contact that you'll do something, set a date and make sure you do it. It's your first test of being reliable.

Cold calling can mean hearing no a lot. Remember that it isn't personal. Getting a yes is as much luck as skill. You need to reach someone who has a need for you and you often have no way of knowing if they do or not. You have to be able to sell yourself; practise so that you can sound professional and confident. Don't put people on the spot, but make sure they know you're interested in working for them.

Networking

Some people love networking, while others would do anything to avoid it. As a freelance editor, you can't afford not to network. You need people to know about you and trust you in order for them to hire you. But you can approach networking in ways that work best for you.

When you are reaching out beyond your comfort zone, take extra care of yourself. Be well rested and prepared before a networking event and give yourself time afterwards to recover your energy.

Face-to-face networking

Opportunities for networking include everything from CIEP local groups to events organised by business support organisations. Conferences organised by editorial organisations, such as the annual CIEP conference, are great places to meet like-minded people and share your experiences and ideas with others. But simply keeping in touch with current or previous clients is an important form of networking, as well.

> ### Tip
>
> Join your local CIEP group. People are very generous with their time and experience, and are more likely to pass on work they can't take on themselves if they've met you (whether online or in person) and you've made a good impression. The friendships developed in local groups can forge strong business links. People share tips and ideas, contact details of potential clients and work opportunities.
>
> If there isn't an active local group in your area, think about setting one up. If you live outside the UK, check out the CIEP's Cloud Clubs.

If you do try face-to-face networking with potential clients, pull out your elevator pitch (see page 6). This is a great opportunity to practise speaking confidently about the services you offer and how they can benefit a potential client. Also be ready to trade business cards or website addresses.

Remember that networking is a two-way process: it's as much about what you can do for others as what they can do for you. For example, if you help one person make a valuable connection with someone else in your network, both people will remember you positively. Later on, either may be able to return the favour with an introduction you need.

3 | Choosing marketing methods that are right for you 23

It's good practice to follow up with a short email or text message when you've connected with someone in person. It helps them remember you and can start a loose, ongoing conversation online. You've put in the effort to go to an event and made initial contact with a potential client or colleague. Make the most of it by taking the next step in growing the relationship.

Of course, this sort of networking can be costly in terms of time, sometimes taking years for work to materialise. Don't give up on contacts you make until you're sure nothing is going to come of it.

Remember that you'll be mingling with people from all sorts of businesses, not just with other editors, and they won't necessarily know what an editor or proofreader is – or even that there's a difference. Listen to what people are asking for, as they might not use the same words to describe what they need. If they talk about needing a 'human spell-check' or a 'sanity check', don't respond with a lengthy discussion of proofreading symbols or Word's Track Changes. Instead, help them understand that what they're looking for is an editor or proofreader.

Social media

There are dozens of social media platforms, and they're changing constantly. Which ones should you join?

Start by thinking about what you want to gain from them. Do you want to connect directly with clients, chatting about your shared topics? Perhaps you want to network with other editors and publishing professionals to share your expertise and referrals. Determine what you're hoping to get out of being on social media and whom you want to connect with.

Next, choose platforms where your desired audience is *and* that you're comfortable using. With so many options, you don't need to feel obligated to be on a social media network that makes you uncomfortable or you don't like using. Find your audience where you're comfortable.

Think carefully about how much time you're going to allocate to these networks. Reports from editorial freelancers vary as to how much direct work they generate, but some people seem to find them useful for passive marketing. In other words, simply having a presence on them and being fairly visible has led to new projects without them ever directly selling their services.

Using social media effectively is all about sharing – being prepared to promote the work, skills and resources of others as well as promoting yourself. All of them allow you to showcase your skills and experience, and to some extent you can design your space in a way that is specific to your business and branding.

> **Tip**
>
> Make sure that whichever of these networks you use, your details are consistent throughout and consistent with other promotional items, such as your website, CIEP Directory entry and CV.

If you're just starting to use social media to market your business, start with just one platform or two at the most. It takes a significant amount of time to build an audience and become comfortable with a platform. Grant yourself that time before adding another platform to your routine.

Online events

Beyond exchanging messages on social media, you might also find opportunities to attend live events online, such as monthly chats for an informal networking group, training sessions in which learners can interact with each other and live video presentations in which attendees can text with each other. Live online events can be wonderful networking opportunities that make distance and (sometimes) time and fees irrelevant. If you struggle to attend in-person events – and even if you don't – take advantage of the relative ease of online events.

> **Tip**
> If you'll be on camera for an online event, be prepared. Test out the best location for you to set up: do you have a space in your office that presents your brand well? Alternatively, check out virtual backgrounds that help you create a professional look. How is the lighting? Video lights can be a great help here. And while you don't need to put on a suit, do spend a little time on your appearance, whether that's an editing-themed T-shirt or a professional-looking top.

Building relationships with your clients

It's also vital to keep in touch with your existing clients. For example, if you're working on a project for them, keep them updated of progress. If you haven't worked for them for a while, drop them a quick email to remind them of you.

It's OK to ask if they have any projects coming up that they need help with, but be careful not to do this too often, to avoid being seen as desperate. Always phrase your messages as helping your client out.

You can also update them on changes to your business that might affect them. Letting them know about an upcoming period when you'll be unavailable or a date when your rates will go up are two good ways to nudge clients to send you projects sooner rather than later.

Consider, too, emailing them about something other than upcoming projects. For example, you might share an article they would benefit from or congratulate them on a milestone or promotion. You'll be focusing on your client in a positive way. You can also do things such as send them a year-end email saying how much you look forward to working with them in the coming year.

If you're in touch with clients regularly, they're more likely to use you or recommend you to colleagues. And should a hiccup appear on a particular project, they're more likely to be understanding if you have a good relationship with them.

Keeping in touch also means that you're more likely to know if they're about to move elsewhere. In such a case you can ask them to take your details to their next position and/or pass your details to whoever is replacing them. This can be a really good way of gaining a new client.

When you finish a project, email your contact to say how much you've enjoyed it and that you'd like to work with them again. If they're impressed with your work they'll be only too pleased not to have to search for someone new for their next project.

This is also a good time to ask them to fill out a short feedback form. This can help you head off problems before you lose a client and give you positive reviews you can use (with permission) in your marketing materials.

Although there's no magic formula to this, be sure to balance staying in touch with not pestering people. If it's been a while since the last project, an email might be called for. For example, if you receive a project from a client about once a quarter and you haven't heard from them in five months, go ahead and email them.

If it's only been a week or two since the last project and you handed the project back with a nudge for more work, then hold off on sending another message. In general, watch for signs of irritation: short responses, terse wording or no response at all could be signs that you're interrupting the client too often. Make a note of it and avoid emailing them for a while.

> **Tip**
> Doing a good job for a fair price and being flexible and easy to work with are strong ways to encourage more work from clients. Clients will be happy to find someone they can trust to deliver what they want, on time and to budget. They want to work with someone who understands them and the work on offer and with whom they feel comfortable. Building rapport that inspires such trust is important.

Word of mouth works wonders, and referrals and recommendations can be among the most powerful marketing tools. These are great ways of getting new clients because they involve no cost to you. But you need to be proactive.

Whenever anyone says anything positive about your work, ask if they would be willing to provide a testimonial for you. The more testimonials you can pull together, the more confident your prospective clients will be of the service you're offering. Put them on your website and in promotional materials. Potential clients can feel quite vulnerable when approaching someone new; when they can see positive feedback from people in their exact role in comparable organisations, they feel more confident about using you.

In editorial freelancing generally, it's rare for us to receive comments on our work – unless it's very bad – and we often don't even see the finished product. So it can be difficult to get feedback or endorsements, and you'll almost certainly have to ask for them. But also make sure you act on any feedback you do get, and take every opportunity to ask clients what they think about your work.

4 | Putting your plan together

By now you're probably suffering from information overload. There are so many techniques, resources and events you can use to promote your services, it may seem like an overwhelming task to get started. Luckily, you don't have to do it all at once.

Your marketing plan will start with the general and move towards specifics. Whether you're writing your first marketing plan or updating an existing one, start with an outline of the information your plan should contain. There are formal templates you can use to create your own marketing plan, but you can as easily create a document that perfectly fits your needs. Use what will work best for you.

> **Tip**
>
> Start small and build on it. If you don't know where to start or don't feel up to setting yourself specific marketing goals, just spend some time thinking about who your ideal clients might be and where they might look for your services. Even vague ideas can evolve and adapt over time into your marketing plan.

Your marketing plan needs to include:

- **Analysis:** where you're at now (**chapter 2**)
- **Goals:** where you want to get to (see below)
- **Strategy:** how you're planning to get there (**chapter 3**)

Start by breaking your goals and strategy down into years (eg this year, next year and three to five years from now). Then break down this year's goals and strategies into quarters, months and even weeks. Consider how much time you can realistically spend each week on your marketing tasks. Marketing is a long game: you need to consistently work at it to see results. While you may see early results, don't let that persuade you that you're done.

When setting your marketing goals, be specific and include how you will measure your progress and a deadline for getting the work done. SMART goals (specific, measurable, achievable, relevant and timely) are a popular way to craft goals you can meet.

Let's say, for example, you want to increase the number of inactive clients who come back to you with work. Your goal might be:

> Persuade three inactive clients to hire me for new work this year by sending emails to three past clients each month and tracking responses on my warm contact sheet.

You can then break down that goal into small tasks:

1. Create a spreadsheet of past clients that includes name, contact information, previous project information and date of the last project. Include space for information on how and when you contacted them, the results and any follow-up plan.
2. Research past clients to identify the ones most likely to rehire you.
3. Write an email or phone script.
4. Set a time each month to reach out. (You could even write the emails ahead of time and schedule them to send at the appointed day and time.)
5. Record your activity.

The bottom line is that you have to know whom you're trying to attract, what you want to accomplish with your marketing efforts and how you're going to let potential clients know you exist. Your marketing plan should address how you plan to:

- retain existing clients (particularly your best 20%)
- encourage your existing clients to use you more often
- find new clients.

It's important not to forget your existing clients when putting together your marketing plan, if only because it costs far less to keep an existing client than to find a new one. An analysis of your client base may well reveal that the 80/20 rule applies: 80% of your income is generated by 20% of your clients. This is not a problem as long as you know which clients make up the 20% so that you can focus your resources and efforts on them.

Your marketing plan doesn't need to be pages and pages long. Write a plan that concisely captures your analysis, goals and strategy. Make it easy to understand and to follow, to encourage yourself to stick with it.

Just recording your plan will make it more likely that you will achieve your goals. Breaking your goals into manageable chunks and setting deadlines will help move you forward.

Need more encouragement? Join an accountability group or partner with colleagues to help everyone meet their short- and long-term goals.

As your business evolves, your marketing plan should evolve with it. It should become almost second nature to review your plan as new avenues open up to you or as old ones become less attractive. Stay up to date on marketing trends and technologies. Try out new things. If they don't work, don't do them again.

Always be thinking about the future. Where will your next projects come from? How do you want to develop your business? Is it time to slow the business down and enjoy retirement? Plan to adapt your business and how you market it to your evolving needs.

5 | Implementing your plan and measuring its effectiveness

Don't let your plan sit and collect dust. Put it to work so you can benefit from the results that constant, consistent marketing brings.

As noted earlier, chunked tasks and deadlines will help you put your plan into action. If you can afford to dedicate an entire day a month to marketing, go for it. If not, define a block of time you can devote to marketing at least weekly and, especially for social media, even daily.

Review your workweek: are there a couple of hours every week when you're least busy? You could start or end your day with an hour of marketing, for example.

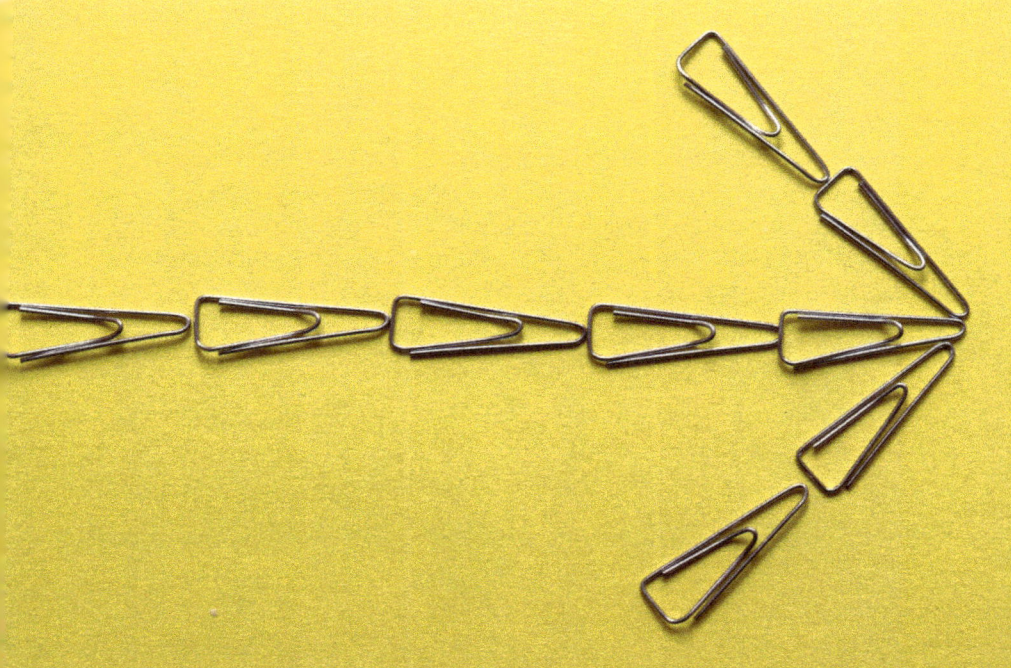

Or maybe Monday mornings are slow for you and you could devote that time to marketing. You might spend 15 or 20 minutes a day participating in the CIEP forums and on social media, just chatting with your connections.

Remember: if you don't take your marketing seriously, making time for it and putting effort into it, you won't see any results.

> **Tip**
>
> You will have times when you're so busy that you don't do the marketing you intended. Paying work has to come first, after all. That's OK. Scale back your marketing tasks and adjust deadlines so that you can keep your business humming along. Just try not to completely stop marketing. And as soon as you can, get back to your regular schedule.

How will you know that your efforts are working? Regularly review the outcome of your marketing efforts. Checking your progress monthly will help you spot issues sooner, but review your results at least quarterly. Maybe you've been marketing your business for years but haven't taken the time to determine how well your efforts are working out for you. Now is a good time to start.

Look at what you've been doing to market your business and measure the results of each effort. Decide whether there are ways you can replicate the positive results your marketing efforts have brought or whether there are some minor (or even major) tweaks you can make to produce better results.

> **Tip**
>
> What if you aren't achieving your goals? What if you discover that you've set a goal that's too high or asks you to do too much at once? As you learn what's achievable, adjust your goals accordingly. Good goals should stretch you, not break you.

5 | Implementing your plan and measuring its effectiveness

It's also important to measure the effectiveness of the different forms of marketing against the cost. Whenever you pay for any form of marketing, record it in a spreadsheet. Try to find out how a client or enquiry came to you and record that in the same spreadsheet, including the income that client brought you. Now you can compare how much an effort costs with how much income it brought you.

Of course, some things have other benefits – such as the social side of networking – that you'll want to take into your calculations as well. If something is expensive and ineffective and doesn't offer any other valuable benefit, cut it from your marketing plan.

Appendix 1 | A basic checklist

1. **Review your business.** Analyse where your business is now: the services you offer, who your clients are, what industries you work in and so on.

2. **Define your goals.** Make your goals clear and easily achievable. Focus on targeting the right people in the right way to maximise results.

3. **Decide whom you're marketing to.** Do you want to get more business from current clients, work from new clients or new business from inactive clients? Consider both market sectors and specific clients.

4. **Create your brand and USP.** Develop your professional image, focusing on what makes you different. What's unique about your service or you as an editor?

5. **Sharpen up your image.** Create the marketing materials you'll use, such as a CV, business cards and a website. You don't need to spend a fortune but do try to make them look professional and update them regularly.

6. **Decide on your marketing methods.** There are so many to choose from; try one or two at a time to avoid becoming overwhelmed. Remember that some clients may need different approaches. Marketing takes time to work, but if a method truly isn't working for you, try something else.

7. **Write up your marketing plan.** It doesn't matter how basic it is. Ensure that it's concise and easy to understand and follow.

Appendix 1 | A basic checklist

8. **Market a little and often.** Don't wait until you're short of work to put your marketing plan into action. It's far better to market yourself a little and often, even when you have enough work. That way you should develop a steady stream of new business.

9. **Review progress regularly.** Look at what's working and what isn't, and refocus your efforts accordingly. Quantify results if possible. Learn from your past experiences: Which marketing tools were effective? Which were unsuccessful? Can you determine why in order to refine and improve next year's marketing strategy?

Appendix 2 | Resources

CIEP resources

CIEP members-only resources: forums, local groups and Cloud Clubs; job adverts and IM Available; The Edit (a bimonthly e-newsletter); spreadsheets and information in Going Solo Toolkit: **ciep.uk/members/going-solo-toolkit**

CIEP website: **ciep.uk** (includes extensive FAQs, fact sheets and recommended book lists)

Littleford, S (2021). **Going Solo: Creating Your Freelance Editorial Business**. 2nd edn. CIEP.

Further learning and advice

Brenner, E (2024). *The Chicago Guide for Freelance Editors: How to Take Care of Your Business, Your Clients, and Yourself from Start-Up to Sustainability*. University of Chicago Press.

Buff, S and Thaler-Carter, RE (2020). *Resumés for Freelancers: Make Your Resumé an Effective Marketing Tool … And More*. Editorial Freelancers Association (EFA).

Freelancers Union blog: **blog.freelancersunion.org**

Louise Harnby (including courses and books on marketing): **louiseharnbyproofreader.com**

Professional directories

Alliance of Independent Authors (ALLi): **allianceindependentauthors.org**

CIEP: **ciep.uk/directory**

Editorial Freelancers Association (EFA): **the-efa.org/hiring**

Editors Canada: **editors.ca/ode/search**

Appendix 2 | Resources

Editors of Color: **editorsofcolor.com/database**

Institute of Professional Editors (IPEd): **iped-editors.org/find-an-editor**

Publishing Training Centre (PTC): **publishingtrainingcentre.co.uk/freelance-finder**

Business support and networking organisations

British Chambers of Commerce: **britishchambers.org.uk**

Business Networking International (BNI): **bni.com**

Chartered Institute of Marketing: **cim.co.uk**

Federation of Small Businesses: **fsb.org.uk**

Small Business (for those in the UK): **smallbusiness.co.uk**

Small Business Administration (for those in the USA): **sba.gov**

Starting a business in Canada: **canada.ca/en/services/business/start.html**

U.S. Chamber of Commerce: **uschamber.com**

About the authors

Erin Brenner is the owner of Right Touch Editing, which provides small and midsized organisations with writing and editing teams. A well-respected industry leader, Erin frequently presents on editing and business topics for editor organisations. Since 2009, she has authored hundreds of blog posts for Right Touch Editing, Visual Thesaurus and others. She is the author of *The Chicago Guide for Freelance Editors: How to Take Care of Your Business, Your Clients, and Yourself from Start-Up to Sustainability*, *Copyediting's Grammar Tune-Up Workbook* and *1001 Words for Success: Synonyms, Antonyms & Homonyms*. When she's not working, she enjoys reading, knitting and hiking. Everything she does is fuelled by tea.

righttouchediting.com

Sara Hulse began her freelance career in 1994 after many years in industry, initially working as a sole trader under the name Technical Text and mainly doing abstracting and copyediting of medical journals. In 2003 she relaunched as a limited company, Write Communications and – while still working mainly on academic STM material – now specialises in natural history, public and environmental health, and architecture. Her PR and marketing experience includes working part-time for the National Trust as a communications officer for almost three years, and six years as the SfEP's marketing and PR director.

Acknowledgements

Revising a work someone else has written is always a daunting task. I'm indebted to Sara Hulse and her informative edition. Time moves on and business practices change. I've done my best to update the information while keeping Sara's excellent structure and all relevant information. Opinions now are a mix of mine and Sara's and are not officially those of the CIEP. I apologise in advance for any errors or omissions and hope that, if there are any, they do not detract from the information provided.

Erin Brenner, September 2023

I am indebted to the many freelance colleagues I have met and chatted to over the years for their examples of good practice, and to the many clients I have worked with for giving me much valuable experience. Together they have provided me with much of the material in this booklet.

I also thank Penny Poole and Krysia Johnson for providing valuable feedback on early versions of the guide.

Sara Hulse, August 2013

www.ingramcontent.com/pod-product-compliance
Lightning Source LLC
Chambersburg PA
CBHW041315110526
44591CB00022B/2920